W9-CFO-440

The Constitution

DAVID & PATRICIA ARMENTROUT

Rourke
Publishing LLC
Vero Beach, Florida 32964

© 2005 Rourke Publishing LLC

All rights reserved. No part of this book may be reproduced or utilized in any form or by any means, electronic or mechanical including photocopying, recording, or by any information storage and retrieval system without permission in writing from the publisher.

www.rourkepublishing.com

PHOTO CREDITS: Cover Scene, Page 33 © North Wind Picture Archives. Cover Document image and Pages 15, 35, 39, 41 Courtesy of the U.S. National Archives and Records Administration. Pages 42, 43 Courtesy of the U.S. National Archives and Records Administration and Earl McDonald. Title Page © PhotoDisc, Inc. Pages 5, 6, 8, 11, 16, 21, 23, 27, from the Library of Congress. Page 12 from the Department of the Interior. Pages 18, 19, 22, 25, 29, 30, 36 from Images of American Political History

Title page: *The Senate and the House of Representatives meet at the Capitol building in Washington, D.C.*

Editor: Frank Sloan

Cover and page design by Nicola Stratford

Library of Congress Cataloging-in-Publication Data

Armentrout, David, 1962-
  The Constitution / David and Patricia Armentrout.
    p. cm. -- (Documents that shaped the nation)
  Includes bibliographical references and index.
  ISBN 1-59515-231-8
  1. United States. Constitution--Juvenile literature. 2. United States--Politics and government--1775-1783--Juvenile literature. 3. United States--Politics and government--1783-1789--Juvenile literature. 4. Constitutional history--United States--Juvenile literature. I. Armentrout, Patricia, 1960- II. Title. III. Series: Armentrout, David, 1962- Documents that shaped the nation.
  E303.A76 2004
  973.4--dc22
                                    2004014415

Printed in the USA
CG

TABLE OF CONTENTS

THE CONSTITUTION OF THE UNITED STATES

A constitution is a set of rules, or laws, that govern a nation, state, or other organized group. The U. S. Constitution is a legal document that spells out the laws and **principles** by which our government must operate. It describes the powers of the government and the rights of the people. It is one of the most important documents in American history.

For more than 200 years, the United States and its system of government have served as a role model for freedom lovers all over the world. The Constitution, written by America's founding fathers, has been used as a guide by nations around the globe looking to secure their own freedoms.

Much of the original plan for the Constitution was written by James Madison. He is sometimes referred to as the father of our Constitution.

James Madison was the fourth president of the United States.

EARLY SETTLEMENTS

North America had been occupied by Native Americans for thousands of years before being discovered by Europeans. The history of European settlement in North America is really quite short in comparison.

But there is no doubt that the arrival of Europeans in North America forever changed the future of the world.

European settlement of North America was slow at first. Christopher Columbus's voyage of 1492 began a time of great exploration of North America. It would be more than 100 years, however, before a lasting settlement was established in what is now the United States. In 1565, the Spanish founded St. Augustine in Florida. It is the oldest continuously occupied city in the United States. The oldest permanent English settlement is Jamestown in Virginia, settled in 1607. The Pilgrims did not arrive from England until 1620, when they established the Plymouth Colony.

Christopher Columbus was a famous European explorer.

Early settlers faced many challenges including long and dangerous sea voyages, disease, starvation, and attack from unfriendly Native Americans. When strong settlements were established that offered protection and eased the difficulty of survival, the European population began to grow.

Once this occurred, settlers began to arrive in much greater numbers from England, France, Holland, Sweden, and Germany.

Settlers came searching for religious freedom, adventure, and economic opportunity. Colonies began to grow and even prosper. European powers saw great potential in the New World. Jealousy and distrust of each other led to a race for control of North America.

Settlers prepare to leave England for the New World.

FIGHTING FOR CONTROL

By the 1680s, Spain occupied Florida, while France controlled Canada (known as New France), and the British claimed colonies along the Atlantic coast. About this time, a series of wars began between France and Great Britain that would continue off and on for nearly 100 years.

Native American tribes were forced to choose sides and took part in many battles, sometimes fighting against each other. The British colonies were not organized and often argued with each other, but their population gave them a big advantage over the French. In 1689, New France had a population of roughly 12,000, while the English colonists numbered more than 200,000.

Great Britain fought many battles such as this one during the French and Indian Wars for control of North America.

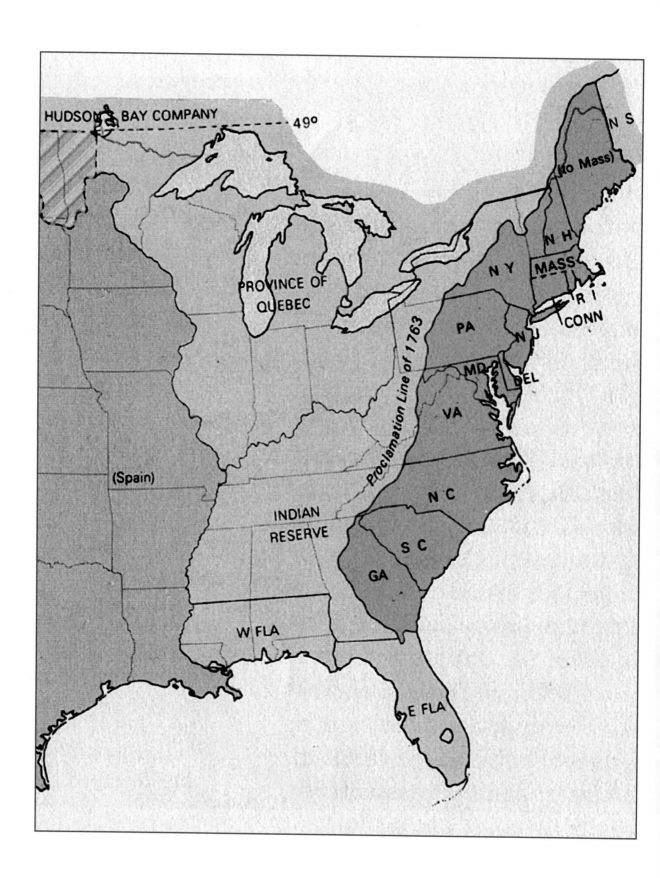

The wars took a heavy toll on everyone involved. France grew weary of the continued fighting and was looking for a way out. Finally, in 1763, an agreement was reached that left Great Britain in control of much of North America. France agreed to give up its claims in North America. Spain, having sided with the French, was forced to trade Florida to Great Britain in exchange for Cuba.

The 13 original American colonies were Virginia, New Jersey, Massachusetts, New Hampshire, Pennsylvania, New York, Maryland, Connecticut, Rhode Island, Delaware, North Carolina, South Carolina and Georgia.

A 1775 map showing the original 13 colonies, British territory, and Spanish territory

THE ROAD TO INDEPENDENCE

The long years of fighting and maintaining the American colonies were very expensive for Great Britain. When the fighting was finally over, Great Britain was left with a large debt. Meanwhile, the American colonies continued to grow by leaps and bounds.

The king of England and the British **Parliament** were looking for ways to pay some of the expense of maintaining America. The most obvious place to look was in the American colonies themselves. The colonies, they reasoned, were receiving protection from their mother country, but were not paying a fair share of the cost. To raise money, British Parliament passed a series of **acts**, or laws, beginning in 1764. The acts taxed the colonies for a variety of products.

By 1770, the colonial population had grown to more than two 2 million.

This illustration published in the 1700s shows citizens of Boston feeling like prisoners under the rule of Great Britain.

The new tax laws did not go over well with the colonists because the colonists had no representation in British Parliament. It seemed to the colonists that they had no legal rights. The colonists insisted that they should be heard.

They told Parliament that *taxation without representation* was not fair. When their complaints were not answered, many colonists begin to organize protests. Protests led to skirmishes between colonists and British soldiers.

Colonial anger with Great Britain grew, and by 1774 many were calling for independence. The unthinkable happened in 1775, when war broke out between the colonies and Great Britain at the battles of Lexington and Concord.

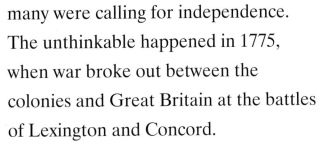

Though freedom became the cornerstone of America's struggle for independence, slavery was common in many of the early colonies. By 1770, there were more than 187,000 slaves in Virginia alone.

The first major battle of the Revolutionary War took place at Lexington, Massachusetts, in 1775.

THE DECLARATION OF INDEPENDENCE

In 1775, a group of representatives from the 13 colonies met to decide what should be done about the conflict with Great Britain. The group, known as the Second Continental Congress, included famous **patriots** such as Samuel Adams, Patrick Henry, John Hancock, John Adams, Thomas Jefferson, Benjamin Franklin, and George Washington. The Congress attempted to resolve the disputes peacefully. When their efforts failed, the American Congress voted to declare independence from Great Britain.

Thomas Jefferson, known for his talent with the written word, was asked to prepare a declaration announcing to the world that the colonies were no longer a part of Great Britain. In the declaration, Jefferson wrote, *"that these United Colonies are, and of right ought to be, free and independent states, that they are absolved from all allegiance to the British Crown, and that all political connection between them and the state of Great Britain is, and ought to be, totally dissolved."*

The Continental Congress approved the final version of the Declaration of Independence on July 4, 1776.

John Adams was a member of the First and the Second Continental congresses and was the second president of the United States.

One of the first jobs presented to the Second Continental Congress was to choose a military leader. George Washington was named as the commander in chief of the Continental Army and took command of colonial forces in Boston on July 3, 1775.

Signing of the Declaration of Independence

CIVIL WAR?

Many colonists who had not made up their minds about independence were moved by Jefferson's words. Though not everyone was convinced that independence was for the best, it was too late to turn back now. Colonists who did not want independence and wished to remain under the rule of Great Britain were called loyalists. Historians estimate that 20 to 40 percent of the colonial population remained loyal to the king. Sometimes family members took opposite sides. One famous example is that of Benjamin Franklin and his son, William. Benjamin Franklin sided with those who wanted independence, while William supported the king. The fighting between countrymen made the Revolution, at least in part, a civil war.

With the decision having been made to seek independence, the Continental Congress was able to turn its attention to fighting a war and building a new nation.

Benjamin Franklin (seated left) was one of five members of the Declaration Committee that helped write the Declaration of Independence.

THE ARTICLES OF CONFEDERATION

War with Great Britain would consume the colonies for the next few years. Congress spent much of its time trying to find ways to pay for the new Continental Army. **Ambassadors** were sent to France, Spain, Holland, and other nations looking for help in America's struggle. But many members of Congress were already looking to the future.

In 1776, Richard Henry Lee, a delegate from Virginia, proposed that Congress prepare a formal constitutional agreement between the colonies. The agreement was called the Articles of Confederation. It would become the first Constitution of the United States. The Articles of Confederation were carefully designed to establish a system of government while limiting the power of federal authority. Congress adopted the Articles of Confederation in 1777. However, the Articles of Confederation did not go into effect until 1781, when the document was officially ratified by all 13 states.

Richard Henry Lee believed the colonies should have a Constitution.

The Articles of Confederation were the first Constitution of the United States of America.

THE WAR IS OVER

After a long and bloody war, Great Britain was beginning to show signs that it was looking for a way out. In 1782, commissioners, or representatives, from the warring nations met in Paris to talk about a deal for peace. The United States sent Benjamin Franklin, John Adams, and John Jay. The commissioners signed a peace treaty. Great Britain agreed to recognize American independence and to withdraw British forces from American territory.

The treaty was presented to the American Congress and ratified on April 15, 1783, officially ending the war.

John Jay helped write the agreement that officially ended the war with Great Britain.

THE CONSTITUTIONAL CONVENTION

It did not take long before the weaknesses of the Articles of Confederation became clear. The colonists had become wary of strong central government under the rule of Great Britain. The authors of the first constitution were careful to limit the power of a central government. In fact, the Articles of Confederation gave Congress so little power that any laws they wrote could be, and often were, ignored.

The Articles of Confederation treated each state almost as if it were its own country. The states agreed the Articles of Confederation were not working. A stronger national government was needed. To talk about the problems faced by Congress, a special meeting, or convention, was called.

The authors of the Constitution framed, or shaped, the document designing it from scratch. That is why they are sometimes referred to as the "framers" of the Constitution.

George Washington was elected as the president of the Constitutional Convention.

The Constitutional Convention met in Philadelphia on May 25, 1787. The delegates at the meeting had been instructed by Congress to consider making changes to the Articles of Confederation. Instead, the delegates set about writing a completely new constitution. Attending the convention were 55 delegates from 12 states. Many of the delegates were lawyers already familiar with law and government. Some were successful merchants familiar with the needs of business. A few owned farms and understood the challenges faced by common people. The gathering included some of the most talented and respected men in America. The background of the men was perfectly suited to the task at hand.

By September, a final **draft** of the document was ready. Of the 42 delegates in attendance, 39 signed their names in approval of the new Constitution. The Constitution was then sent to Congress, and the meeting of the Constitutional Convention was closed.

The Constitution was drafted at Independence Hall in Philadelphia.

Rhode Island did not send any delegates to the Constitutional Convention.

THE NEW CONSTITUTION IS RATIFIED

Congress received the Constitution by the end of September 1787. Some members of Congress were not happy that the delegates at the Constitutional Convention had written an entirely new constitution. Still, there was enough support for the Constitution that Congress agreed to present it to the states.

In order to pass the new Constitution, it was necessary for at least 9 of the 13 colonies to ratify it. On June 21, 1788, New Hampshire became the ninth state to ratify the Constitution, and in so doing made it official. On July 2 Congress announced there was a new Constitution. Plans were made for a new government as described by the Constitution. New York City was named the temporary capital.

September 17 is known as Constitution Day because this is the day delegates to the Constitutional Convention met for the last time to sign the document they had created.

Signing of the United States Constitution

THE PREAMBLE

The opening sentence of the U.S. Constitution is called the preamble. The preamble explains the reasons a new government was formed:

We the people of the United States, in order to form a more perfect union, establish justice, insure domestic tranquility, provide for the common defense, promote the general welfare, and secure the blessings of liberty to ourselves and our posterity, do ordain and establish this Constitution for the United States of America.

The authors of the Constitution were clear that they wanted the people of the United States to enjoy justice, peace, the ability to defend themselves against enemies, and freedom. The government would work for the people rather than the other way around.

Thirty-nine delegates signed the new Constitution.

ARTICLES OF THE CONSTITUTION

There are 4,543 words in the Constitution, with the Articles making up the largest section. The articles of the Constitution describe the way in which the government will insure the goals set forth by the preamble. There are seven articles in all. Some articles needing further explanation are divided into sections.

The first three articles divide the government into three separate branches, while the last four articles deal with other concerns.

The Constitution creates a system of government with "checks and balances." Each branch of the government has some control over the decisions made by another. This insures that no single branch can become too powerful.

The Constitution was drafted in less than 100 days.

Article I-The Legislative Branch

The first branch of government is the Legislative branch, called Congress. Congress is further divided into two groups: the House of Representatives and the Senate. Each state has representatives in both the House of Representatives and the Senate. Members of Congress are elected by the people from the state they represent. Congress makes the laws of the United States.

Article II-The Executive Branch

The second branch is the Executive branch, or the presidency. The president must carry out the laws of Congress. The president is also the commander in chief of the United States military.

Article III-The Judicial Branch

The Judicial branch of government consists of the federal court system including the Supreme Court. The Judicial branch interprets, or explains, the laws of Congress and the Constitution.

Article IV-The States

Article IV forces each state to honor the laws of all other states.

The meeting room of the House of Representatives

Article V - The Amendment Process

The framers of the Constitution knew that as times changed, the need for new laws would arise. Article V explains the rules that must be followed to change, or amend, the Constitution.

Article VI - Legal Status of the Constitution

Article VI makes it clear that the Constitution of the United States "shall be the supreme law of the land."

Article VII - Ratification

The final article states that the "new" Constitution would become official when 9 out of the 13 states had ratified, or voted, in favor of it.

The average age of the delegates to the Constitutional Convention was 44. Benjamin Franklin was the oldest at 81 years of age.

The last page of the Constitution and the signatures of the delegates

AMENDMENTS

The ink on the parchment had barely dried when amendments to the Constitution were proposed. Some complained that the Constitution did not provide enough protection of individual rights. Under the rules of Article V in the Constitution, ten amendments were soon added. These first ten amendments are called the Bill of Rights.

Since the Constitution was **ratified**, 27 amendments have been added to the document. Just as the framers had envisioned so long ago, the ability to make changes would insure that the Constitution remained one of the most important documents in American history.

The Bill of Rights is made up of the first ten amendments to the Constitution.

PRESERVING THE CONSTITUTION

In July of 2001, the U. S. Constitution was removed from public display as part of a major restoration project called the Charters of Freedom Re-encasement Project. The Charters of Freedom are the Declaration of Independence, the Constitution, and the Bill of Rights.

The restored Charters of Freedom are now on public display.

After removing the documents from their encasements, scientists examined the condition of the Constitution. They painstakingly checked every letter for damage and cleaned and treated the **parchment**. The National Institute of Standards and Technology built special cases to house the Charters of Freedom. Five cases preserve the four pages of the Constitution and its transmittal page, signed by George Washington. The cases are filled with argon gas, which will protect the documents from environmental damage. The Charters of Freedom were put back on display at the National Archives in Washington, D.C., in September of 2003.

Conservators check every detail of the Constitution.

TIME LINE

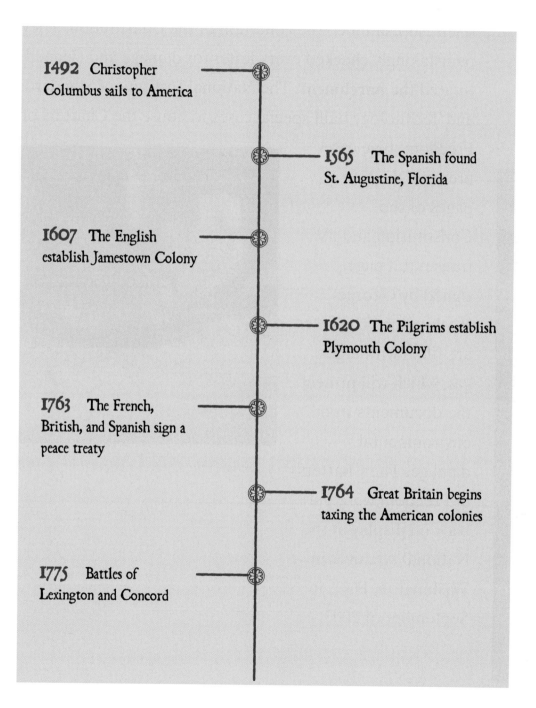

1492 Christopher Columbus sails to America

1565 The Spanish found St. Augustine, Florida

1607 The English establish Jamestown Colony

1620 The Pilgrims establish Plymouth Colony

1763 The French, British, and Spanish sign a peace treaty

1764 Great Britain begins taxing the American colonies

1775 Battles of Lexington and Concord

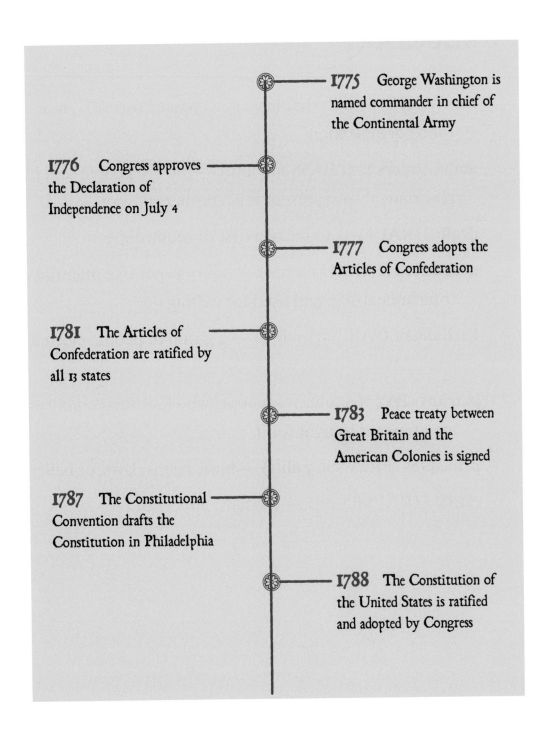

1775 George Washington is named commander in chief of the Continental Army

1776 Congress approves the Declaration of Independence on July 4

1777 Congress adopts the Articles of Confederation

1781 The Articles of Confederation are ratified by all 13 states

1783 Peace treaty between Great Britain and the American Colonies is signed

1787 The Constitutional Convention drafts the Constitution in Philadelphia

1788 The Constitution of the United States is ratified and adopted by Congress

GLOSSARY

acts (AKTS) — bills that have been passed formally by a ruling organization

ambassadors (am BASS uh durz) — the top people sent by a government to represent it in another country

draft (DRAFT) — to make a first or rough copy

parchment (PARCH muhnt) — heavy paper like material made from animal skin and used for writing

Parliament (PAR luh muhnt) — a group of people elected to make laws

patriots (PAY tree uhtz) — people who love their country and are prepared to fight for it

principles (PRIN suh puhlz) — basic truths, laws, or beliefs

ratified (RAT uh fyed) — officially approved

FURTHER READING

Murray, Stuart. *American Revolution.* DK Publishing, 2002.
Nardo, Don. *The U.S. Constitution.* KidHaven Press, 2002.
Sobel, Syl. *The U.S. Constitution and You.*
   Barron's Educational Series, Inc., 2001.

WEBSITES TO VISIT

www.archives.gov/national_archives_experience/constitution.html
www.americanrevwar.homestead.com/files/INDEX2.HTM
www.constitutionfacts.com/

ABOUT THE AUTHORS

David and Patricia Armentrout have written many nonfiction books for young readers. They have had several books published for primary school reading. The Armentrouts live in Cincinnati, Ohio, with their two children.

INDEX